Micronutrient Diet Recipes

(A Beginner's Guide)

The ultimate guide to losing weight, regaining energy and live a healthy lifestyle in 28 days.

By

DAVE SCOTT

*M*icronutrient Diet Recipes

Copyright © 2019: by DAVE SCOTT

ISBN-13: 978-1-950772-33-9
ISBN-10: 1-950772-33-0

All Rights Reserved. No part of this publication may be reproduced in any form or by any means, including scanning, photocopying, or otherwise without prior written permission of the copyright holder.

Disclaimer:

The information provided in this book is designed to provide helpful information on the subjects discussed. The publisher and author are not responsible for any specific health or allergy needs that may require medical supervision and are not liable for any damages or negative consequences from any treatment, action, application or preparation, to any person reading or following the information in this book.

Micronutrient Diet Recipes

Table of Contents

INTRODUCTION 6
   THE MICRONUTRIENT MIRACLE 6

THE MICRONUTRIENT MIRACLE RECIPES MADE SIMPLE 7
   15 DELECTABLE MICRONUTRIENT LOW FAT RECIPES 7
      Light Asparagus Strata 7
      Low Fat Beef, Pinto Bean and Sweet Corn Chili 9
      Chocolate Crinkles 11
      Herbed Zucchini and Mushroom Frittata 13
      Low Fat Mini Meatloaves 16
      Low Fat Potato Latkes 18
      Quinoa-Stuffed Peppers 20
      Sausage and Mushroom Brunch Casserole 22
      Savory Spring Bread Pudding 24
      Shepherd's Pie 27
      Low Fat Southwestern Burgers 30
      Low-Fat Thumbprint Cookies 32
      Low Fat Turkey Gravy 34
      Low Fat Cranberry Orange Muffins 35
      Low Fat Crêpes 37
   15 DELECTABLE MICRONUTRIENT LOW CARB RECIPES 39
      Cincinnati Chili 39
      Low Carb Sugar-Free Pumpkin Vanilla Chia Pudding 42
      Low-Carb Four-Bean Salad 43
      Low-Carb Asian Noodle Dish with Pork 45
      Low-Carb Barbecue "Baked" Beans 47
      Sugar-Free Cole Slaw 48
      Lasagna in a Bowl 50

Micronutrient Diet Recipes

Low-Carb Pasta with Chicken and Roasted Red Pepper Sauce 52

Low-Carb Shrimp and "Grits" 54

Low-Carb Tamale Pie 57

Mexican Grilled Chicken Marinade 59

Chicken Masala 60

Slow Cooker Thai Peanut Chicken 62

Turkey and Asparagus Roll Up Casserole Recipe 64

15 DELECTABLE MICRONUTRITION GLUTEN FREE RECIPES 67

Chicken Tacos to Die For 67

Creamy Tomato Soup 69

Crock Pot Barbecue Ribs 70

Crockpot Beef Stew 71

Easiest Crockpot Beef Ever 73

Paleo Pulled Pork Recipe 75

Crock Pot Roasted Chicken Recipe 76

Slow cooker "pepper steak" roast 77

Slow Cooker Pot Roast with Shallots and Baby Carrots 78

Slow Cooker Roast, Potatoes, and Carrots 79

Slow cooker Crabapple & Pepper Jelly 82

Strawberry Lavender Chia Jam (Pectin & Sugar Free) 83

15 DELECTABLE MICRONUTRIENT VEGAN RECIPES 84

Scrambled Eggs with Avocado, Onion and Cheddar 84

Edamame Salad with Avocado and Radishes 85

Avocado and Chickpea Salad Sandwiches 87

Vegan Twist on the Classic Tuna Sandwich 89

Mango Avocado Salad 90

Avocado and Cucumber Salad with Cilantro-Ginger Dressing 91

Tuscan White Bean Soup 93

Mushroom soup with White Beans 95

Chickpeas Simmered in Masala Sauce 97

Fingerling Potato Salad with Green Chili-Cilantro Salsa 99

Five-minute vegan pancake 100

Roasted Cauliflower & 16 Roasted Cloves of Garlic.. 101

Roasted Green Beans 102

Vegetarian Lasagna 103

Vegetarian Split Pea Soup 104

CONCLUSION 106

Thanks 107

INTRODUCTION
THE MICRONUTRIENT MIRACLE

The Micronutrient Miracle reveals how our habits deplete essential micronutrients and provides an easy, prescriptive plan to reverse these effects. It has been discovered that our poor health and growing waistlines can be traced back to the hidden crisis of a micronutrient deficiency. Statistic has it that more than 90 percent of all Americans are deficient in at least one of these health-promoting vitamins and minerals and don't even know it.

According to the celebrity Nutritionists Jayson B. Calton Ph.D. and Mira Calton CN vitamins and minerals essential for optimum health-- are being stripped from our diet and depleted by our lifestyle habits. And it meant to know that these deficiencies cause today's most common illnesses.

The Mircronutrient Miracle, is an incredible cure-all program, which can help you lose weight and prevent and reverse common disorders, including obesity, heart disease, and diabetes.

However, Mira herself developed advanced osteoporosis at the age of 30. But with the help of Jayson's, she was able to reverse her disease through micronutrient therapy.

This book (micronutrient diet cookbook) is complete with cutting-edge science and success stories, it will appeal to a wide variety of readers, regardless of their preferred dietary profile, including low-carb, low-fat, vegan, and even Paleo options.

THE MICRONUTRIENT MIRACLE RECIPES MADE SIMPLE

15 DELECTABLE MICRONUTRIENT LOW FAT RECIPES

Light Asparagus Strata

TIPS:

1. This version of strata contains a blend of eggs and egg substitute, uses nonfat milk and reduced fat cheese and also uses whole wheat bread for an extra nutritional boost.
2. You can make this stratum the night before or a few hours ahead if it's more convenient for you. If so, I suggest you simply cover and refrigerate the strata until about a half hour before you want to bake it.

Ingredients

3 large eggs

2 cups of nonfat milk

1 ½ teaspoons of Dijon mustard

3 ounces of shredded reduced-fat extra-sharp cheddar

8 slices of whole wheat bread (cut into fourths)

¾ cup of liquid egg substitute

2 tablespoons of chopped chives

Freshly ground black pepper

¾ pound of fresh asparagus (trimmed and cut into small pieces)

Preparation

1. Meanwhile, you heat oven to a temperature of 350 degrees.
2. After which you spray bottom of an 11 by 7 baking dish with nonfat cooking spray.
3. After that, you place half the bread pieces in the baking dish, overlapping as needed.
4. At this point, you whisk eggs, egg substitute, milk, chives and mustard in medium bowl.
5. Then you pour half the egg mixture over the bottom layer of bread.
6. This is when you scatter about half the asparagus pieces on top, then add the rest of the bread pieces.
7. Furthermore, you pour remaining egg mixture on top, followed by the remaining asparagus pieces.
8. After which you press down to ensure the bread is soaked by the egg mixture.
9. In addition, you sprinkle with cheese.
10. Finally, you bake in an oven for about 45-50 minutes, until golden and when a knife inserted in the middle comes out clean.

NUTRITIONAL INFORMATION

Per Serving:

Calories 186

Total Fat 6.3g (sat 3.5g),

Cholesterol 88mg

Sodium 333mg

Carbohydrate 18.8g

Fiber 2.9g

Protein 13.5g

Low Fat Beef, Pinto Bean and Sweet Corn Chili

Tips:
1. Enjoy this recipe by itself or on a small bed of whole grain rice.
2. This recipe is quick and easy for even the busiest of weeknights.

Ingredients

2 small green pepper (chopped)

2 tablespoons of chili powder

1 pound of extra-lean ground beef or turkey

3 cups of frozen sweet corn

2 medium onion (finely chopped)

2 jalapeno or Serrano Chile (finely chopped)

4 teaspoons of cumin

2 (15-ounce) can crushed tomatoes

2 (15-ounce) can pinto beans

Preparation

1. First, you spray a large nonstick skillet with nonstick cooking spray.
2. After which you sauté onion, green pepper and Chile pepper over a medium heat, until onions have softened.
3. After that, you add chili powder, cumin and cook for 2 minutes until fragrant.
4. Then you crumble ground beef or turkey and cook until no longer pink.
5. At this point, you empty can of tomatoes, pinto beans and sweet corn into meat mixture and simmer for about 10-15 minutes.
6. Enjoy!

NUTRITIONAL INFORMATION

Per Serving:

Calories 309

Total Fat 5g (sat 1.9g)

Sodium 229mg

Carbohydrate 47.9g

Fiber 8.8g

Protein 8.4g

Chocolate Crinkles
1. **Tips:**
    The secret to these soft chocolaty delights are to refrigerate the dough for at least 4 hours, and to roll them in plenty of powdered sugar before baking.
2. Remember, the dough will still be somewhat sticky when you begin to scoop it, so I suggest you use two spoons to drop each spoonful into the powdered sugar, and roll it once before picking it up and forming a rounder ball.

Ingredients

1 ½ cups of sugar

2 large eggs

2 teaspoons of vanilla extract

2 teaspoons of baking powder

2/3 cup of powdered sugar (sifted)

1 cup of unsweetened cocoa powder

½ cup of canola oil

4 egg whites

2 cups of all-purpose flour

½ teaspoon of salt

Preparation

1. First, you use an electric mixer, mix cocoa powder, sugar and oil in a large bowl.
2. After which you add egg and mix again, followed by egg whites.
3. After that, you add vanilla extract and mix until blended.
4. Then whisk flour, baking powder and salt in a small bowl.

Micronutrient Diet Recipes

5. At this point, you stir flour mixture into cocoa mixture.
6. This is when you cover with plastic wrap and refrigerate for at least 4 hours and when it is ready to bake, preheat oven to 350 degrees.
7. After that, you line 4 large baking sheets with parchment paper.
8. Furthermore, you place sifted sugar into a small bowl.
9. After which you drop dough by the teaspoonful into powdered sugar and roll it once.
10. In addition, you pick up the piece of dough and form a ball.
11. Then you place sugar-covered dough balls about 1 ½ inches apart on baking sheet.
12. Finally, you bake each sheet separately for about 10-12 minutes, or together, transferring half way through.

Note: this will make about 72 chocolate crinkles.

NUTRITIONAL INFORMATION

Per Cookie:

Calories 54

Fat 1.8g (sat 0.2g)

Cholesterol 6mg

Sodium 31mg

Carbohydrate 8.5g

Fiber 0.5g

Protein 1g

Herbed Zucchini and Mushroom Frittata

Tips:

1. Enjoy this low fat recipe when you want to prepare a special breakfast or brunch dish.
2. Remember, it is perfect for Easter or Mother's Day (NOTE: you can use egg substitute to lower the amount of cholesterol, but you can also use a combination of whole eggs and egg whites if you prefer).

Ingredients

¾ cup of sliced mushrooms

¼ cup of fat-free milk (or better still fat-free half and half)

½ teaspoon of dried oregano

¼ cup of reduced fat cheese

1 small-medium zucchini (halved lengthwise then sliced)

1 cup of egg substitute (or preferably 2 whole eggs and four egg whites)

Freshly ground black pepper

2-3 small sprigs fresh rosemary

Preparation

1. First, you coat a medium nonstick skillet with an oven-proof handle with cooking spray.
2. After which on a medium heat, you sauté mushrooms and zucchini until softened, about 3-4 minutes.
3. Meanwhile, heat broiler.
4. After that, you combine egg substitute (or better still whisk eggs and egg whites) with milk, ground pepper and oregano.
5. Then you pour mixture over vegetables in skillet.

6. At this point, you add rosemary sprigs, and sprinkle with cheese.
7. Furthermore, you cook gently for five minutes, until eggs set around the edges.
8. This is when you carefully transfer skillet to broiler and cook frittata under the broiler for about 3-4 minutes until eggs are set and are golden in color.
9. Make sure you remove skillet using a potholder, as the handle will get very hot.
10. In addition, you cut frittata into 4 wedges and serve immediately.
11. Finally, if your skillet doesn't have an oven-proof handle, wrap the handle in foil.

NUTRITIONAL INFORMATION

Per Serving (with egg substitute):

Calories 60

Fat 1.5g (sat 0.9g)

Cholesterol 5mg

Sodium 183mg

Carbohydrate 3.2g

Fiber 0.5g

Protein 8.8g

NUTRITIONAL INFORMATION

Per Serving (with eggs and whites):

Calories 83

Fat 4g (sat 1.7g)

Cholesterol 110mg

Sodium 154mg

Carbohydrate 2.8g

Fiber 0.5g

Protein 9.4g

Low Fat Mini Meatloaves

Tips:

1. These low fat recipes are a big hit with my kids and are also good for them, too, as they're made from extra-lean ground beef and packed with shredded veggies.
2. You can enjoy these low fat mini meatloaves with skinny mashed potatoes and seasonal vegetables.

Ingredients

2 medium carrot (shredded)

1 yellow onion (finely chopped)

2 tablespoons of chili powder

2 slice of whole grain bread as breadcrumbs

2/3 cup of tomato ketchup

2 pounds of extra-lean ground beef

2 medium zucchini (shredded and squeezed dry)

1 green pepper (finely chopped)

4 tablespoons of Worcestershire sauce

4 egg whites

Preparation

1. Meanwhile, you heat oven to a temperature of 400 degrees.
2. After which you lightly spray a nonstick or silicone muffin pan with nonstick cooking spray.
3. After that, you crumble ground beef into a large bowl.
4. At this point, you add shredded carrots and zucchini, and chopped onion and green pepper.

5. Then you add chili powder, Worcestershire sauce, breadcrumbs and stir with a fork.
6. Furthermore, you add egg whites and stir again with a fork until well blended.
7. After which you knead the mixture with your hands but sometimes this makes the meat overly tough.
8. In addition, you spoon mixture into prepared muffin pan, and top each cup with ketchup.
9. Finally, you bake for about 25 minutes, making sure that the internal temperature reaches 165 degrees.

NUTRITIONAL INFORMATION

Per Serving:

Calories 150

Fat 4.2g (sat 2g)

Cholesterol 47mg

Sodium 98mg

Carbohydrate 9.2g

Fiber 2.3g

Protein 18.7

Low Fat Potato Latkes

Tips:

1. To make this recipe crispy, I suggest you squeeze out as much moisture as you can, and preheat the cookie sheet before placing the latkes on it.
2. You can enjoy these low fat potato latkes with fat-free sour cream and some home-made applesauce.

Ingredients

1 medium onion

Freshly ground black pepper

1 ½ pounds Yukon Gold (or preferably Russet Potatoes)

¼ cup of flour

2 egg whites

Preparation

1. Meanwhile, you heat oven to a temperature of 450 degrees.
2. After which you peel, cut and shred potatoes and onion, using either a grater or a food processor.
3. After that, you place a large cookie sheet in hot oven.
4. At this point, you empty shredded potatoes and onion into a colander and squeeze out as much excess moisture as you can.
5. This is when you transfer potato and onion mixture to a large bowl.
6. Then you add flour, egg whites and black pepper, and combine well with a fork.
7. Furthermore, you remove cookie sheet from oven and coat with nonstick cooking spray
8. After which you form 2-2 1/2-inch flattened rounds with the potato mixture and place on hot cookie sheet.

9. Finally, you return cookie sheet to oven and cook for about 7-8 minutes each side, until crisp and golden.
10. It makes about 12-15 latkes.

NUTRITIONAL INFORMATION

Per Serving:

Calories 192

Fat 0.5g (sat 0g)

Cholesterol 0mg

Sodium 39mg

Carbohydrate 41.1g

Fiber 3.8g

Protein 6.6g

Quinoa-Stuffed Peppers

Tips:

1. These recipe makes a nice low-fat meatless entree or side dish.
2. In the other hand, quinoa is a wonderful choice for those who can't eat gluten, plus it makes a nice change from rice or meat-filled peppers.
3. However, if you want to make 1 cup of cooked quinoa, you'll need 1/2 cup of quinoa, rinsed, then cooked in 1 cup of water or broth for extra flavor.
4. After which you make sure your broth is gluten free if you are feeding this to someone who has a gluten problem.
5. Remember, if you prefer your peppers to be softer still, I suggest you bake them for about 10 minutes or so longer.

Ingredients

4 teaspoons of canola oil

4 garlic cloves (minced)

3 cups of diced cremini mushrooms

1 cup of fat-free, low-sodium vegetable broth

1 cup of chopped fresh parsley

4 large red or yellow bell peppers (halved lengthwise, stem intact)

2 medium onion (finely chopped)

4 medium carrots (diced)

2 cups of cooked quinoa

2 cups of chopped baby spinach

Preparation

1. Meanwhile, you heat oven to a temperature of 400 degrees.
2. After which you steam or simmer bell peppers in a large pot for about 5 minutes until slightly soft.
3. After that, you heat oil in medium skillet and gently sauté onions, garlic and carrots on medium-low heat until softened.
4. Then you add mushrooms and cook until soft.
5. At this point, you stir in cooked quinoa.
6. Furthermore, you add broth, spinach and parsley and cook for about 2 minutes.
7. After that, you scoop one fourth of the quinoa mixture into each bell pepper half, packing firmly.
8. This is when you place peppers in a baking dish.
9. In addition, you cover the bottom of the dish with ½ cup of water.
10. Finally, you cover with foil and bake for about 30 minutes, until filling is hot.

NUTRITIONAL INFORMATION

Per Serving:

Calories 198

Fat 4.2g (sat 0.3g)

Cholesterol 0mg

Sodium 50mg

Carbohydrate 33.3g

Fiber 6.7g

Protein 6.6g

Sausage and Mushroom Brunch Casserole

1. **Tips:**
   This recipe saves fat calories by using chicken sausage, liquid egg substitute in place of some of the eggs, and reduced fat cheese.
2. You can also use whole grain bread for added fiber.
3. Remember that the end result still remains a delicious breakfast or brunch dish the whole family can enjoy.
4. Feel free to prepare this casserole ahead of time, refrigerate overnight and bake in the morning.

Ingredients

1 teaspoon of canola oil

1 garlic clove (smashed)

8 ounces of sliced mushrooms

1 cup of liquid egg substitute

1 tablespoon of Dijon mustard

Dash salt and pepper

6 slices sliced whole wheat bread (crusts removed)

1 onion (chopped)

8 ounces' chicken sausages (casings removed)

2 large eggs

1 cup of fat free milk

2/3 cup of shredded sharp cheese (divided)

Preparation

1. Meanwhile, you heat oven to a temperature of 350 degrees.

2. After which you cut bread into fourths and lay at the bottom of an 11 X 7 baking dish coated with nonstick cooking spray.
3. After that, you heat oil in large skillet on medium heat.
4. At this point, you cook onions and garlic until onions have softened, about 5 minutes.
5. Then you crumble chicken sausage meat into skillet; add mushrooms, and cook for about 5 minutes until the meat has browned.
6. This is when you whisk together eggs, egg substitute, milk, mustard, 1/3 cup of cheese and seasoning.
7. Furthermore, you pour over bread in baking dish.
8. After which you top with sausage and mushroom mixture.
9. In addition, you add remaining cheese.
10. This is when you cover and refrigerate the casserole overnight and bake in the morning.
11. Finally, you bake for about 45-50 minutes at 350 degrees Fahrenheit until puffy and golden.
12. Then you let rest for about 10-15 minutes before serving.

NUTRITIONAL INFORMATION

Per Serving:

Calories 202

Fat 6.1g (sat 2g)

Cholesterol 66mg

Sodium 465mg

Carbohydrate 21.9g

Fiber 3.5g

Protein 15.8g

Savory Spring Bread Pudding

Tips:

1. However, for best results, I suggest you use stale bread (a day or two old).
2. I say Italian here, but note that any artisanal bread will work beautifully.
3. Remember, a whole wheat sourdough would be perfect, as well as adding a little extra fiber.

Ingredients

2 cups of fat-free half and half

1 cup of fat-free, low-sodium chicken broth

Freshly ground black pepper

1 cup of sliced leeks

½ cup of fresh (chopped parsley)

½ cup of reduced-fat sharp cheddar cheese (it is optional)

1-pound day-old Italian loaf (chopped into 1-inch cubes)

2 eggs (lightly beaten)

Dash salt

1 tablespoon of olive oil

8 ounce of pack sliced mushrooms

1 pound of fresh asparagus (cut into 1 1/2 inch pieces)

Preparation

1. Meanwhile, you heat oven to a temperature of 375 degrees
2. After which you spray a 9 x 13-inch baking pan with nonstick cooking spray.
3. After that, you place bread cubes in a large bowl.

4. At this point, you combine fat-free half and half, eggs, chicken broth and seasonings in a quart pitcher or bowl.
5. Then you pour liquid over bread cubes.
6. This is when you stir to coat the bread.
7. Furthermore, you set aside to allow liquid to soak in.
8. After that, you heat oil on medium in a large skillet.
9. Then you add leeks, chopped asparagus and sliced mushrooms.
10. In addition, you sauté for about 3-4 minutes.
11. At this point, you turn heat to low and cover for about 2 minutes.
12. This is the point you uncover, and stir in chopped parsley.
13. After which you fold asparagus, leeks and mushrooms into bread mixture, then transfer to prepared baking pan.
14. Finally, you sprinkle with shredded cheese if using, and bake for about 35-40 minutes.

Per Serving (with cheese):

Calories 270

Fat 5.6g, (sat 1.5g)

Cholesterol 56mg

Sodium 461mg

Carbohydrate 41.8g

Fiber 3.8g

Protein 13.2g

Per Serving (without cheese):

Calories 256

Fat 3.3g (sat 0.9g)

Cholesterol 54mg

Sodium 411mg

Carbohydrate 41.6g

Fiber 3.8g

Protein 11.2g

Shepherd's Pie

Tips:

1. Remember this a low fat take on a classic English dish and it was traditionally made with leftover meat (usually lamb or beef).
2. This recipe can be made ahead and frozen for later use (for me I often prepare it one day and use it the next).
3. However, if you want to reduce the fat content further, I suggest you use only 3/4 pound of beef and add an extra cup of vegetables--more peas or some sweet corn.

Ingredients

2 medium onion (finely chopped)

2 pound of extra-lean ground beef

4 tablespoons of no-salt-added tomato paste

2 cups of frozen peas

2 tablespoons of canola oil

4 large carrots (chopped)

4 tablespoons of Worcestershire sauce

4 teaspoons of dried mixed herbs

2 cups of fat-free, reduced sodium beef broth

Ingredients for the Topping:

2 tablespoons of light butter

4 pounds Yukon Gold potatoes (peeled and cut into 1-1 1/2-inch pieces)

1 cup of fat-free milk

Preparation

1. First, you heat in a large pot canola oil on medium-low heat.
2. After which you sauté onions and carrots until softened.
3. After that, you turn up heat to medium-high and add beef; cook until no longer pink.
4. Then you add Worcestershire sauce, tomato paste, herbs and broth.
5. At this point, you reduce heat and simmer uncovered for about 15 minutes.
6. Furthermore, you add peas, then simmer for 5 minutes more.

Note: If sauce seems too watery for your liking, I suggest you combine 1 teaspoon of cornstarch into 1/8 cup of water and stir into beef mixture.

7. Then while sauce is simmering, you bring a large pot of water to boil.
8. After that, you add potatoes, reduce heat to a simmer and cook until tender, about 15-20 minutes.
9. In addition, you drain water and add milk and light butter.
10. After which you mash with a potato masher until smooth (you can season if you like).
11. At this point, you pour sauce into an 11-inch by 7-inch baking dish and allow to cool slightly.
12. Then you top with potato (Optional: feel free to sprinkle with 1/3 cup reduced-fat cheese).
13. Finally, you bake in a preheated 400-degree oven for about 20-25 minutes.

NUTRITIONAL INFORMATION

Per Serving (without cheese):

Calories 322

Fat 7.6g (Sat 2.8g)

Cholesterol 49mg

Sodium 260mg

Carbohydrate 41.2g

Fiber 5.7g

Protein 22.5g

Low Fat Southwestern Burgers

Tips:

1. Remember, that these tasty, low fat burgers use extra-lean ground beef combined with mashed black beans to reduce fat content and make moist, flavorful patties.
2. However, the jalapeno pepper, cumin and cilantro add a nice little kick.
3. Make sure you use a hotter Chile pepper if you prefer, or omit it altogether if you want a subtler flavor.
4. You can serve burgers on a whole grain or sourdough bun with plenty of low fat condiments (NOTE: fresh salsa and low fat sour cream work perfectly).

Ingredients

½ cup of minced red onion

4 teaspoons of ground cumin

½ cup of tomato sauce

4 tablespoons of fresh chopped cilantro

2 cups of reduced-sodium black beans (rinsed)

2 jalapeno pepper (seeded and finely chopped)

1 ½ pounds of extra-lean ground beef

2 egg whites

Preparation

1. First, you mash black beans in a small bowl with a fork.
2. After which you add onion, jalapeno pepper, cumin and mix well.

Micronutrient Diet Recipes

3. After that, you place ground beef in a large bowl, followed by the bean mixture.
4. Then you add sauce, egg white and cilantro.
5. At this point, you blend well with a fork.
6. Furthermore, you form into four 3/4-inch patties.
7. Finally, you broil or grill for about 5-6 per side until internal temperature reaches 160 degrees.

NUTRITIONAL INFORMATION

Per Serving:

Calories 145

Fat 4.4g (sat 2.2g)

Cholesterol 52mg

Sodium 173mg

Carbohydrate 5.9g

Fiber 1.7g

Protein 20.4g

Low-Fat Thumbprint Cookies

Tips:

1. You will find these little cookies irresistible.
2. If you trying to make these cookies low fat, I still firmly believe a little butter is necessary with these (as for me I used just a ¼ cup).
3. You can enjoy these little cookies with a cup of nonfat cocoa.
4. Remember, this is the perfect cookie recipe for kids to make.

Ingredients

1 cup of light brown sugar (firmly packed)

2 teaspoons of vanilla extract

1 cup of good-quality raspberry jam

½ cup of butter (softened)

2 eggs

3 cups of all-purpose flour

½ teaspoon of salt

Preparation

1. Meanwhile, you heat oven to a temperature of 350 degrees.
2. After which you line a large cookie sheet with parchment paper or a silicone mat.
3. After that, in a large bowl you cream butter and brown sugar together using an electric mixer.
4. Then you add egg and vanilla, and mix until blended.
5. At this point, you whisk together flour and salt in a small bowl.
6. This is when you gradually add flour to wet ingredients, and mix with a wooden spoon, forming a large ball.

7. If the dough is sticky, I suggest you refrigerate for an hour before proceeding.
8. Otherwise, I may suggest you go ahead and form 1-inch balls and place them 1-inch apart on the cookie sheet, making a deep thumbprint in the center of each.
9. Finally, you bake for about 10 minutes.
10. Then you remove from oven and after one minute, place on a wire rack to cool.
11. Make sure you add a little raspberry jam to the center of each cookie.

NUTRITIONAL INFORMATION

Per Cookie:

Calories 101

Fat 2.6g (sat 1.5g)

Cholesterol 17mg

Sodium 37mg

Carbohydrate 17.8g

Fiber 0.4g

Protein 1.4g

Low Fat Turkey Gravy

Ingredients

½ cup of flour

Ground black pepper to taste

Pan juices from turkey

8 cups of fat free, reduced sodium chicken broth

8 tablespoons of red wine

Preparation

1. First, while your cooked holiday turkey is resting, I suggest you strain the pan drippings and pour into a gravy separator.
2. After which you place roasting pan on stovetop over a medium heat (NOTE: you will likely need two burners).
3. After that, you sprinkle flour into pan and stir until golden brown.
4. Then you reduce heat to low and return defatted drippings to pan, add chicken broth and wine.
5. At this point, you stir with a whisk until blended.
6. Furthermore, you turn heat back up to medium and cook, stirring constantly, until gravy thickens.
7. This is when you season with black pepper if desired.
8. Finally, you pour into a gravy boat, ready to serve

Low Fat Cranberry Orange Muffins

Tips:

1. Remember that low fat muffins can be light and tender (make sure you spoon the flour gently into the measuring cups and level with the back of a knife).
2. However, you should resist the temptation to scoop the cups into the flour and pack them full.
3. These delicious recipes have just the right balance of sweetness and tartness.

Ingredients

1 teaspoon of baking powder

½ teaspoon of salt

1 large egg (lightly beaten)

2/3 cup of orange juice

2 cups of fresh cranberries (chopped)

2 cups of all-purpose flour

½ teaspoon of baking soda

1 cup of sugar

¼ cup of canola oil

2 teaspoons of grated orange zest

Preparation

1. Meanwhile, you heat oven to a temperature of 400 degrees.
2. After which you line muffin pan with paper muffin cups.
3. After that, you combine in a large bowl the flour, baking powder, baking soda, salt and sugar.
4. At this point, you combine with a whisk.

5. Then in a small bowl, you add beaten egg, oil, orange juice, zest and stir well.
6. Furthermore, you make a well in the flour mixture and add wet ingredients.
7. After which you stir until just moist, being careful not to over mix.
8. Finally, you fold in chopped cranberries and spoon batter into prepared muffin pan.
9. Then you bake for about 16-18 minutes, until muffins are golden and spring back when touched.

Makes 12 muffins.

NUTRITIONAL INFORMATION

Per Muffin:

Calories 204

Fat 5.1g (sat 0.4g)

Cholesterol 18mg

Sodium 196mg

Carbohydrate 36.4g

Fiber 1.4g

Protein 2.9g

Low Fat Crêpes

Tips:

1. Crêpes as you may know are thin pancakes which can be eaten in the same way as pancakes or rolled up with a filling of your choice.
2. However, these are the exact kind of "pancakes" I used to flip on Shrove Tuesday when I grew up in England.

Ingredients

½ teaspoon of salt

1 ½ cups of nonfat milk

1 cup of all-purpose flour

2 eggs (lightly beaten)

Preparation

1. First, you gently spoon flour into measuring cup and level with the back of a knife.
2. After which you put flour and salt in a medium bowl and stir with a hand whisk.
3. After that, you make a well in the center of the flour mixture and add egg.
4. At this point, you whisk egg and flour while pouring milk into bowl, stirring well to combine (NOTE: The batter should be free of lumps).
5. Then you let stand for about 5 minutes.
6. Furthermore, you spray an 8-inch nonstick skillet with nonstick cooking spray.
7. After which you heat skillet on medium high and then add a 1/4 cup of batter to hot skillet and swirl around the pan to cover as much of the bottom of the skillet as possible.

8. As the edges cook, I suggest you use a spatula to lift the edges of the crêpe and then after about 1 minute, flip the crêpe over and cook for a further 30 seconds.
9. This is when you transfer to a plate and start over until the batter is done.
10. This should yield about 12 crêpes, so probably serves 4 or 6.
11. Feel free to enjoy these recipes with a sprinkling of confectioners' sugar and a squeeze of lemon, or use the crêpes as the base for a fruity filling.

NUTRITIONAL INFORMATION

Per Crêpe:

Calories 57

Fat 0.9g (sat 0.3)

Cholesterol 35mg

Sodium, 122mg

Carbohydrate 9.3g

Fiber 0.3g

Protein 3g

15 DELECTABLE MICRONUTRIENT LOW CARB RECIPES

Cincinnati Chili

Tips:
Remember that Cincinnati chili shares many of the basic ingredients with Texas chili, it is seasoned and cooked quite differently, as it originated from a Greek stew.

Ingredients

1 medium onion (chopped finely)

3 tablespoon of chili powder (it all depends on the heat of the powder and your taste)

1/8 teaspoon of cloves

1 tablespoon of paprika

1 oz. unsweetened chocolate

1 Tablespoon of beef Better than Bouillon (or better still 3 bouillon cubes)

¼ Cup of red wine (it is very optional and very non-traditional)

2 lbs. of ground meat (I prefer half turkey and half beef)

4 cloves garlic (or better still 2 teaspoons garlic powder)

1 teaspoon of allspice

2 teaspoons of cinnamon

1 tablespoon of Worcestershire Sauce.

2 bay leaves

1 (15 oz.) can tomato sauce

1 tablespoon of red wine vinegar (it is optional and traditional)

Preparation

However, the meat for the chili was boiled instead of browned. This will give it a different consistency (NOTE: the pieces of meat are very small and separated - no clumps).

1. Remember that most recipes I've seen do brown the meat with the onions, though. Let me introduce to you the way I do it, which is kind of a cross between the two:

    First, you put the meat and onions in a stock pot or large deep frying pan, and cook for 5 minutes.
2. After which you add about 2 cups of water and mix and chop with a spatula until the hamburger is pretty well broken up.
3. After that, you add the rest of the ingredients and simmer for about 45-60 minutes.
4. Remember, correcting the seasoning at the end is very essential.
5. Cincinnati chili is not supposed to be super-spicy, feel free to add heat if you like, or a little vinegar to perk up the flavor, or salt, or a bit of sweetener if it's harsh.

However, in Cincinnati, you can have it as above with or without cheese and/or onions. Or you can have:

Two-way chili on spaghetti (I prefer spaghetti squash) or
Three-way chili on spaghetti with cheddar cheese or
Four-way chili on spaghetti with cheese and onions or
Five-way chili all of the above, plus kidney beans

NUTRITIONAL INFORMATION

Serving Size: EACH OF 8 SERVINGS.

Calories: 240

Fat: 13g

Carbohydrates: 6g

Dietary fiber: 2.5g

Protein: 23g

Low Carb Sugar-Free Pumpkin Vanilla Chia Pudding

Ingredients

2/3 cup of chia seeds

1 teaspoon of pumpkin pie spice

6 full dropper's vanilla liquid stevia

2 cups of unsweetened almond milk

1 cup of canned pure pumpkin (not pie filling), plus 4 tablespoons

1 teaspoon of vanilla extract

Directions:

1. First, you mix all ingredients together in a bowl except the extra 4 tablespoons of pure pumpkin.
2. Then once combined well, you pour into 4 serving glasses.
3. After that, you spread one tablespoon pure pumpkin over the top of each pudding.
4. Finally, you refrigerate for 10 minutes until set.
5. You can top with Diary Free Whipped Cream if desired.

NUTRITIONAL INFORMATION

Serving Size: PER SERVING.

Calories: 220

Fat: 14.7g

Carbohydrates: 20.9g

Dietary fiber: 16.2g

Protein: 9.4g

Low-Carb Four-Bean Salad

TIPS:

1. This low-carb recipe is sugar-free and the beans are less starchy ones.
2. Remember, if you want to use kidney beans or chick peas instead of the black soy beans or edamame, I suggest that it is preferable not to use canned beans, which are more glycemic and have less resistant starch than if you buy the dry beans and soak and cook them yourself.
3. However, if you want a three-bean salad, I suggest you use 16 oz of the green beans and eliminate one of the others.

Ingredients

1 (15 oz) can yellow string beans (**NOTE:** if you can get frozen or fresh, all the better)

1 cup of fresh or better still frozen shelled edamame (fresh soy beans)

1/3 cup of chopped green Bell pepper

¼ cup of chopped fresh parsley

1 teaspoon of prepared mustard

1 teaspoon of dried herbs (I prefer Greek or Italian mixtures, but thyme is good – so feel free to use whatever you like)

½ cup of light olive oil or any preferred oil

12 oz. of green beans - fresh or frozen (feel free to use canned if you prefer)

1 (15 oz) can of black soy beans

1/3 cup of chopped

¼ cup of red onion (chopped)

3 tablespoons of red wine vinegar

½ teaspoon of garlic powder

Salt and pepper (to taste)

Preparation

1. First, you combine the beans, peppers, onion, and parsley in a large bowl.

   After which you mix the vinegar with the mustard and seasonings, either in a small bowl, or a shaker such as a glass jar.
2. After that, you add the oil, and whisk or shake to combine.
3. Then you pour over the beans and vegetables, and toss.

Note the direction on oil:

The problem with using extra-virgin olive oil is that it tends to solidify when refrigerated.

In the other hand, if the salad is going to be eaten all in one sitting, or if you're willing to let it come to room temperature before eating, I suggest you use extra-virgin if you want.

Another alternative to it is a high-mono type of safflower or sunflower oil such as Saffola brand. NOTE: I'm not a fan of using other seed oils such as corn oil or soy oil as they are so high in omega-6 fats.

NUTRITIONAL INFORMATION

Serving Size: PER SERVING.

Calories: 144

Carbohydrates: 3g

Dietary fiber: 4g

Protein: 5g

Low-Carb Asian Noodle Dish with Pork

Tips:

However, this low-carb noodle dish can be made with shirataki noodles or tofu noodles.

Chicken can be used to substitute pork.

Remember that this recipe has a passing similarity to Dan Noodles.

Ingredients

1 lb. of ground pork

¼ cup of dry sherry

1 tablespoon of rice vinegar or better still cider vinegar (note rice vinegar can be sugary)

8 cloves garlic (minced, pressed, or grated)

2 Tablespoons of sesame oil

6 green onions or preferably scallions (chopped)

1-2 Tablespoons of mild oil (such as peanut or high oleic safflower oil)

2 (12 oz) of packages shirataki or better still tofu noodles

½ cup of soy sauce

1/3 cup of peanut butter

½ teaspoon of Asian chili sauce (or preferably other hot sauce)

2 Tablespoons of grated fresh ginger

1 lb. of bean sprouts

Pepper

Preparation

Micronutrient Diet Recipes

1. First, you mix ground pork, 2 Tablespoons of the soy sauce, and the sherry together, and set aside.
2. After which you mix the rest of the soy sauce with the peanut butter, vinegar, and hot sauce together, although with ¼ cup water.
3. After that, you heat skillet or wok until hot.
4. Then you add peanut or other mild oil to the pan and cook pork, breaking it up into small bits as it cooks.
5. In the meantime, you rinse noodles in hot water in a colander, and cut them up into shorter pieces with kitchen or regular scissors (for me I just stick my scissors in and cut a few times.)
6. Furthermore, when meat is brown, you add the ginger and garlic, and cook another minute or so, until fragrant.
7. At this point, you add sauce mixture, and the noodles.
8. After which you toss together and heat through.
9. In addition, you add bean sprouts and toss again.
10. Finally, you sprinkle top with scallions.

Low-Carb Barbecue "Baked" Beans

Tip:

1. Remember that this recipe uses black soy beans for great taste with fewer carbs and more protein in it.
2. This recipe also uses my low carb barbecue sauce.

Ingredients

2 cups of low carb barbecue sauce

2 can of black soy beans

2 small onions (chopped fine)

Preparation

1. First, you sauté onion in a little oil until soft.
2. After which you add the beans and the sauce.
3. Then you simmer for about 15-20 minutes.

NUTRITIONAL INFORMATION

Serving Size: PER SERVINGS.

Calories: 166

Carbohydrates: 9g

Dietary fiber: 7g

Protein: 11g

Sugar-Free Cole Slaw

1. **Tips:**
   However, I like to season this coleslaw dressing with Penzey's Buttermilk Ranch Seasoning, and it's almost as good.
2. Remember, this recipe is great with barbecue or any grilled food and the cold creaminess is great up against hot BBQ spices.

Ingredients

2/3 cup of sour cream

Artificial sweetener to equal 2 Teaspoons of sugar

1 teaspoon of onion powder

¼ teaspoon of black pepper

1 lb. cabbage (shredded)

1/3 cup of mayonnaise

2 Tablespoons of lemon juice

1 teaspoon of garlic powder

1/8 teaspoon of paprika

¼ teaspoon of plus one pinch salt

Preparation

1. First, you mix all Cole slaw dressing ingredients together, and then mix them into the cabbage.
2. Then you balance the lemon juice and sweetener to your own taste.

NUTRITIONAL INFORMATION

Serving Size: PER SERVINGS.

Calories: 145

Carbohydrates: 4g

Dietary fiber: 2g

Protein: 2g

Lasagna in a Bowl

Ingredients

Ground meat, cooked and drained (NOTE: 1 lb. makes about 6 servings)

Per Serving:

½ cup of sugar-free spaghetti sauce

1 cup of cooked spaghetti squash (or better still other low carb pasta alternative)

1/3 cup of ricotta cheese

¼ cup of shredded mozzarella cheese

2 tablespoons of parmesan cheese

Preparation

1. First, you cook the "pasta alternative", be it spaghetti squash or something else.

   After which you cook the meat with salt and pepper to taste.
2. After that, you drain off the fat.
3. You can combine the sauce and the meat at this point, if you wish.

   At this point, you heat the ricotta (NOTE: microwave works best)

Your layer in bowl:

Pasta alternative

Ricotta cheese

Ground meat

Mozzarella

Sauce

Parmesan.

NUTRITIONAL INFORMATION (WITH SPAGHETTI SQUASH)

Serving Size: PER SERVINGS.

Calories: 435

Carbohydrates: 19g

Dietary fiber: 3g

Protein: 38g

Low-Carb Pasta with Chicken and Roasted Red Pepper Sauce

TIPS:

1. Remember, that this recipe can use any kind of low-carb pasta, but I prefer to use shirataki fettuccini noodles.
2. However, it can be a nice change from tomato sauce on pasta.

Ingredients

1 ½ lbs. of boneless skinless chicken (cut into cubes for 5 servings and less for fewer servings)

Salt and pepper to taste

Basil (It is optional - fresh chopped preferred)

Low-carb pasta (NOTE: if you using shirataki noodles, two 8 ounce packages works well for 4 servings)

½ cup of onion (finely chopped)

Roasted Red Pepper Cream Sauce

Preparation

1. First, you season the chicken with salt and pepper.
2. After which you sauté' chicken and onions in a small amount of oil until cooked through.
3. After that, you heat Roasted Red Pepper Sauce through in a saucepan or in the microwave (NOTE: Do not boil).
4. At this point, you rinse shiratake noodles in hot water (or prepare other low carb pasta).
5. Then you cut with kitchen shears to desired length.
6. Finally, you toss ingredients together (**NOTE:** if fresh basil is available, I will usually chop some up and add it at this point).

NUTRITIONAL INFORMATION

Serving Size: EACH OF 5 SERVINGS.

Calories: 302

Carbohydrates: 4g

Dietary fiber: 2.5g

Protein: 33g

Low-Carb Shrimp and "Grits"
1. **Tips:**
   This recipe is a low-carb version of the delicious South Carolina classic.
2. Remember that "grits" are made with almond meal, so are much more filling than regular grits.

Ingredients

Salt

¼ teaspoon of cayenne pepper (or better still ½ medium-hot red pepper such as New Mexico)

1 cup of almond meal

¼ teaspoon of salt

4 pieces of thick-cut bacon

2 tablespoons of whiskey (it is optional but tasty! - Irish, bourbon, and Canadian whiskeys all work well)

1 pound of large raw shrimp, peeled and deveined (preferably thaw if frozen)

Pepper

1 packet of sweetener

1 cup of water

1 cup of grated sharp white cheddar cheese

1/3 cup of minced shallot (feel free to use onion plus one clove garlic, but it isn't as good!)

½ cup of red Bell pepper (chopped to small dice)

Micronutrient Diet Recipes

Optional garnish: finely chopped green onion, chopped parsley, or chopped chives

Preparation

1. First, you sprinkle shrimp with salt, red pepper, pepper, and packet of sweetener.
2. After which you put in refrigerator.
3. Then if you want to make the "grits", you first mix the almond meal, salt and water in a saucepan (NOTE: a whisk works well for this).
4. After that, you bring to a boil and cook for about 1-2 minutes, until the mixture thickens somewhat (it will thicken more as it cools).
5. After which you remove from heat and whisk in the cheese.
6. Then you let sit for a minute or so until the cheese fully melts, then whisk again.
7. At this point, you fry the bacon, and remove from the pan (NOTE: Also remove all but a tablespoon of the bacon grease).
8. Furthermore, you fry the shallot over medium-low heat, until soft but not brown.
9. This is when you add red pepper and sauté for about 1-2 minutes, until it just begins to soften.
10. After which you remove from pan.
11. In addition, you raise heat to medium-high.
12. After that, you add another tablespoon of the bacon grease to the pan and heat until a shrimp placed in the grease sizzles immediately.
13. Then you add the shrimp, and cook them about a minute on each side and if using whiskey, I suggest you turn off heat and add it to the pan.
14. At this point, you stir until most of the liquid is gone, which should not take long!

15. Finally, you add vegetables and bacon to pan and heat until the mixture is hot.
16. Make sure you serve over "grits", and garnish if desired.

NUTRITIONAL INFORMATION

Serving Size: PER SERVINGS.

Calories: 490

Carbohydrates: 6.5g

Dietary fiber: 3.5g

Protein: 39g

Low-Carb Tamale Pie
Ingredients
1 ½ lbs. of ground beef (I prefer 20% fat for the calculations)

1 small red Bell pepper (or better still ½ large)

1 can tomatoes, chopped (about 15 oz.)

Salt and pepper

½ raw onion, chopped

1 small green Bell pepper (or better still ½ large)

2 tablespoons of chili powder (or to taste)

1 small can of ripe olives, chopped (about 4 oz.)

Crust
½ cup of plain whey protein powder

¼ cup of juice from the tomatoes

¼ teaspoon of turmeric

1 cup of shredded cheddar cheese (or better still Mexican blend)

½ cup of almond meal

1 egg

¼ teaspoon of chili powder

¼ teaspoon of salt

Preparation
1. First, you heat oven to a temperature of 350° F.
2. After which you drain the tomatoes, and save the juice.

3. After that, you put the onion and the beef into a large skillet, and cook on medium-high heat, breaking up the beef as it cooks.
4. Then when some of the fat from the beef begins is rendered out, then you add the green and red peppers, and the chili powder.
5. At this point, you cook until the beef is cooked through.
6. Furthermore, you add the drained tomatoes and the olives, and cook for another minute.
7. Add salt to taste.
8. After that, you mix the ingredients for the crust together, except for the cheese.
9. This is when you pour the beef and vegetables into a 9 X 13-inch pan, and pour the batter for the crust over the mixture.
10. In addition, you sprinkle the cheese on top.
11. Finally, you bake for about 15-20 minutes, or until crust begins to brown.
12. As for me, I usually cut it up into 12 squares, with 2 squares making a serving.

NOTE: If you want to reduce calories, I suggest you pour off some of the fat.

NUTRITIONAL INFORMATION

Serving Size: EACH OF 6 SERVINGS.

Calories: 498

Carbohydrates: 6.5g

Dietary fiber: 3.5g

Protein: 34g

Mexican Grilled Chicken Marinade

Ingredients

½ cup of water

½ teaspoon of hot powdered Chile (such as cayenne)

2 teaspoons of dried thyme

Pinches of cloves

2 teaspoons of garlic powder

1 cup of oil, olive or better still other

½ cup of lime juice

4 tablespoons of powdered ancho chills (or better still other mild chiles)

2 teaspoons of oregano

4 teaspoons of cinnamon

3 teaspoons of salt

6 tablespoons of sugar substitute

Preparation

1. First, you mix lime juice and water, and then whisk all the other ingredients, ending with the oil.
2. THEN you marinate chicken for about 4 to 6 hours before grilling.

NOTE: however, it is so hard to know with a marinade how much of it actually ends up on what you're eating, but I can't imagine this adds significant carbohydrates to the chicken. Let say about 1 gram per serving at the very most.

Chicken Masala

Ingredients

2 small onion

6 tablespoons of (or so) olive oil

Chicken broth (or better still Better than Bouillon)

2 lb. of boneless skinless chicken breasts

2 cups of mushroom slices

1 cup of dry Masala wine

4 tablespoons of minced Italian (flat leaf) parsley

Preparation

1. First, if you desired, pound chicken between two pieces of wax paper or plastic (NOTE: use anything from an old wine bottle to a small heavy pot for this).
2. After which you season chicken with salt and pepper.
3. After that, you heat oil in skillet and add chicken.
4. At this point, you cook until done, remove, and cover with foil.
5. Then you add onion and mushrooms, cook until soft.
6. Furthermore, you add wine to pan and cook for 1 to 2 minutes.
7. This is when you judge the amount of liquid for sauce for chicken.
8. Remember, if you need more, you add a bit of broth.
9. After that, you taste, and adjust seasonings and if it needs more salt, this is a good time to add a little Better than Bouillon, if you have it, for the chicken flavor and salt.
   Finally, you pour vegetables and sauce over chicken, and sprinkle with parsley.

NUTRITIONAL INFORMATION

Serving Size: FOR 3 SERVINGS EACH HAS.

Calories: 336

Carbohydrates: 3g

Dietary fiber: 1g

Protein: 36g

Slow Cooker Thai Peanut Chicken

NUTRITIONAL INFORMATION

Servings (NOTE: It does not include bean threads)

Serving Size: 1/2 Cup

Calories: 196

Fat: 7 g

Carbohydrates: 2 g

Fiber: 1 g

Sodium: 120 g

Sugar: 0 g

Protein: 30 g

Ingredients

¾ cup of light coconut milk (canned)

1 tablespoon of peanut butter, with no sugar added

2 tablespoons of chopped peanuts, with no sugar added

4 (about 8 oz. each) chicken breasts, boneless, skinless, raw

4 sticks dried lemongrass

1 lime (zest and juice)

Directions

1. First, you pour the light coconut milk in to the slow cooker.
2. After which you use a whisk, to blend in the peanut butter until it is well dissolved in the milk.
3. After that, you place the chicken breasts in the milk.

4. Toss in the lemongrass and add the lime juice and zest over the top. (Reserve the peanuts for after cooking)
5. Then you cook on low for about 4 hours or until the chicken reaches an internal temperature of at least 165 degrees.
6. Furthermore, when you finished cooking, shred the chicken with two forks and stir in the peanuts.
7. Finally, you eat as it is or serve over a bed of bean threads as we did here (NOTE: cooked to package directions)

Tips:

Remember that Thai food typically has some kick to it (I did not add any hot spices for personal reasons). Nevertheless, you can certainly stir in some cayenne or other pepper to give it that kick that most people expect.

Turkey and Asparagus Roll Up Casserole Recipe

NUTRITIONAL INFORMATION

Serving size: 3 Roll-Ups

Calories: 425

Fat: 24g

Carbohydrates: 12g (10g net carbs)

Sugar: 0g

Sodium: 1983mg

Fiber: 2g

Protein: 41g

Ingredients

<u>Ingredients for the Cheddar Sauce</u>

4 tablespoons of cream cheese (diced at room temperature)

Salt and white pepper (to taste)

½ cup of heavy cream

½ cup of cheddar cheese (shredded)

¼ teaspoon of dry mustard

<u>Ingredients for the Casserole</u>

1¼ pound of asparagus spears (fresh or frozen, thawed and drained)

Dried parsley

1 pound of deli turkey breast (sliced medium)

Cheddar Sauce (get the recipe above)

1-2 Roma tomatoes (or better still about 4 cherry tomatoes)

Micronutrient Diet Recipes

Directions:

Directions for the Cheddar Sauce

1. First, you warm the cream in a medium saucepan over medium-low heat.
2. After which you add the cream cheese and whisk well until melted.
3. After that, you add the cheddar cheese about one tablespoon at a time, letting it melt before whisking in more.
4. Then you stir in the mustard, salt, and pepper and whisk well one last time.

Directions for the Casserole

1. Meanwhile, you heat the oven to a temperature of 350° F while you are constructing the casserole.
2. After which you clean and trim asparagus to the desired length.
3. After that, you take 2 asparagus spears and roll them up in 1 slice of the deli turkey.
4. Then you place the turkey and asparagus roll in a baking dish, seam side down.
5. At this point, you repeat the procedure with the remaining turkey and asparagus until both are all used up.
6. Furthermore, you pour the Cheddar Sauce over the turkey and asparagus rolls, and use a spatula to smooth it out and distribute it evenly.
7. This is when you slice the tomatoes thinly and place them on top of the sauce.
8. After that, you sprinkle the top of the casserole with a bit of dried parsley to add some additional color to the dish.
9. Then you bake for about 30-40 minutes, or until everything is hot and bubbly.
10. Make sure you serve immediately with steamed broccoli spears and a nice, Spinach Salad with Strawberries.

Notes

1. Remember that this recipe can easily be doubled.
2. However, it reheats well, and can also be made up to 24 hours ahead of time and baked at the last minute.
3. Feel free to substitute ham for the turkey. Or, if you want to turn this into a company breakfast casserole by placing sliced hard-boiled eggs on top in addition to the tomatoes.

15 DELECTABLE MICRONUTRITION GLUTEN FREE RECIPES

Chicken Tacos to Die For

Ingredients

6 chipotle chili peppers in adobo sauce (if you want more of a punch, I suggest you add more chilies)

4 cups of salsa (or preferably a 30 oz. can have chopped stewed tomatoes)

4 cinnamon sticks

Taco shells (you can omit for a GAPS legal meal)

4 lbs. of chicken breast (bone in or bone out, cus I actually used some of each)

2 large onion (sliced)

4 cloves of garlic

Salt to taste

DIRECTIONS:

1. First, you place chicken breasts in a crockpot, (there is no need to defrost if frozen).
2. After which you pour in the tomatoes.
3. After that, you mix in the chipotle chilies and adobo sauce, garlic and cinnamon sticks.
4. At this point, you top with the slices of onion (NOTE: I give it a bit of a stir to make sure the chicken is coated).
5. This is when you cook on high for about 4 hours (and low for 8).
6. Remember that you'll want the meat to be tender enough to just fall off the bone.
7. Then you remove the chicken pieces, chipotle peppers and cinnamon sticks.

8. Furthermore, you shred the chicken, for me, I do this using two forks.
9. After that, you throw out the peppers and cinnamon (note: you can chop the peppers up and leave them in the mix, but it will be hotter).
10. Then you put the chicken back in the crockpot with all the yummy juices and mix thoroughly.
11. Remember, this tastes great on tacos or as a taco salad.
12. Finally, you add your favorite taco toppings like cheese, sour cream, more salsa and salad.

Creamy Tomato Soup

Ingredients

1 small onion (diced)
1-2 large carrots (diced)
1 Tablespoon of basil or to taste. (**NOTE:** Fresh basil will be better tasting, but dried can be used as well).
Freshly grated parm cheese (for your topping)

28 oz. of diced tomatoes (please try not to use canned tomatoes if at all possible due to BPA) you may also use fresh or frozen tomatoes

1-2 stalks of celery (diced)

4 cups of chicken broth (preferably homemade)

8oz of cream (preferably from grass fed cows)

1- 1 ½ teaspoons of sea salt

Directions:

1. First, you combine tomatoes, celery, onion, carrots and chicken broth in crockpot.
2. After which you cook on low for 8 hours or high for 5 until veggies are soft.
3. After that, you puree with an immersion blender until smooth.
4. At this point, you add basil, cream and salt.
5. Then you cook for another hour.
6. Finally, you top with a generous portion of grated parmesan cheese when serving.

Crock Pot Barbecue Ribs

Ingredients:

1 onion

Garlic powder

Baby back ribs (use as many as you can fit in the slow cooker)

Homemade barbecue sauce

A pinch of salt and pepper

Preparation:

1. First, you slice the onion and set it at the bottom of the slow cooker pot.
2. After which you sprinkle ribs with just a pinch of salt and pepper and a little bit of garlic powder.
3. After that, you generously rub meat with barbecue sauce and set on top of the onions.
4. Then you cook on high for about 4-6 hours, until ribs are tender.
5. Meanwhile, you heat oven broiler.
6. At this point, you transfer ribs to a cookie sheet and broil until brown or slightly charred.
7. Finally, you top with more warm barbecue sauce and serve.

Crockpot Beef Stew

Ingredients:

3 pounds of grass fed beef stew meat (cut into 1-inch pieces)

2 tablespoons of homemade taco seasoning (or preferably other similar spice blend)

4 tablespoons of unsalted butter

5 tablespoons of arrowroot

3 tablespoons of organic tomato paste

1 teaspoon of dried oregano (preferably non-irradiated)

¼ teaspoon of ground allspice

1 ½ cups of diced carrots

Garlic cloves, should be smashed and coarsely chopped, as many as you like (it is optional)

Handful of chopped fresh parsley (it is optional)

2 tablespoons of extra virgin olive oil

2 teaspoons of coarse sea salt

1/2-1 teaspoon of cracked black pepper

10 ounces' button mushrooms (thinly sliced)

4-5 cups homemade veal or better still beef stock (at room temperature)

1 teaspoon of dried thyme (preferably non-irradiated)

1 teaspoon of dried basil (preferably non-irradiated)

1 ½ pounds of potatoes, cut into a small dice (you can substitute turnips if needed)

1 ½ cups of frozen pearl onions, thawed OR better still onion diced

1 cup of frozen green peas (thawed)

Directions:

1. First, you set the beef out and bring to room temperature.
2. After which you toss in a bowl with olive oil, salt, pepper and seasoning.
3. After that, you heat some lard in a large cast iron skillet over medium high heat.
4. Then you brown the beef on all sides in two batches.
5. At this point, you add the butter, veal stock, mushrooms, flour, tomato paste, herbs, spices, and browned meat to a slow cooker.
6. Furthermore, you cover the crockpot and set the temperature to high.
7. After that, you cook for 1 hour after which you add the potatoes, carrots and onions (if using fresh diced onions) and continue to cook the stew for another 7 hours.
8. Then during the last hour of cooking, you add the pearl onions (if using) and replace the lid.
9. Once the stew is cooked, you stir in the peas and parsley and serve immediately.
10. If you want to make this a GAPS friendly stew, I suggest you omit the arrowroot and potatoes and use turnips.
11. On the other hand, if you want to make a thicker gravy remove cooked turnips with some broth and puree until a thick paste.
12. Finally, you add back into the stew and stir (NOTE: Make sure you do this before the last hour of cooking).

Easiest Crockpot Beef Ever

Ingredients:

Homemade Beef Stock

1 grass fed chuck roast (about 1.5 -3 pounds)

For the Taco Seasoning

6 teaspoons of chili powder

5 teaspoons of cumin

2 teaspoons of sea salt

1/8 teaspoon of cayenne

5 teaspoons of paprika

3 teaspoons of onion powder

1 ½ teaspoons of garlic powder

Directions:

1. First, you cut your roast into approximately 1 inch cubes with poultry or kitchen shears.
2. After which you leave all the fat intact.
3. After that, you place in your crock-pot on low and add just enough stock to barely cover the bottom of the crock.
4. Then you add the taco seasoning (remember that 1 recipe is enough for 1-2 pounds of meat).
5. At this point, you turn your crock-pot on low and let it cook all day.
6. For me, I cook mine for about 7-8 hours.

NOTE: It will be very tender and moist and easily fall apart.

7. Furthermore, you pull it apart a bit more with forks so it is like pulled beef.

8. Finally, you serve this meat with sprouted corn tortillas fried in lard, some lacto-fermented salsa and raw cheese or cultured cream. Or better still over top of mashed cauliflower or in a taco bowl.

Paleo Pulled Pork Recipe

Crock pot (this is the one I used)

2 large onion

½ cup of yellow mustard

1 teaspoon of all-spice

2 cups of pureed tomato

1 cup of beef or better still chicken broth (try to make your own)

8-10 lb. of pork shoulder roast (preferably pastured)

6 cloves of garlic

½ cup of maple syrup

2 tablespoons of salt

Cream from the top of 2 can (about 13.5 oz each can) of coconut milk

Directions:

1. First, you dice onion and mince garlic.
2. After which you combine all ingredients in the crock pot and mix well (except for the roast).
3. After that, you set crockpot to "low" and then use a skillet to sear the roast on all sides on medium high heat.
4. At this point, you place the roast in the crockpot for about 6-8 hours.
5. Then after about 6 hours or so shred the pork with a fork (it should shred easily) and mix with the sauce that has formed in the crockpot.
6. Finally, you serve and enjoy!

Crock Pot Roasted Chicken Recipe

This recipe is quick, easy, nutritious and delicious (NOTE: It is nice and moist and the meat falls off the bone).

Ingredients

1 onion (white or yellow)

1 teaspoon of Thyme

1 teaspoon of Sage

½ teaspoon of Pepper

1 whole chicken (remove giblets and neck and use for stock)

6-8 cloves of garlic (sub 1-2 Tablespoons of Garlic Powder)

1 teaspoon of Rosemary

1 teaspoon of Tarragon

½ teaspoon of Salt

Directions:

1. First, you remove the chicken from the package, removing neck and giblets for use in stock and rinse chicken in cold water.
2. After which you roughly chop onion and stuff it into the cavity of the chicken.
3. After that, you slice garlic cloves and insert between the skin and the meat of the chicken.
4. Then you combine seasoning and rub onto the chicken.
5. At this point, you place everything in the Crock pot on high for 4-6 hours (NOTE: It should be done cooking in 4 hours but the longer it cooks the more tender it will be).
6. Finally, you throw in veggies of your choice when you are cooking then dinner is done! So simple.

Slow cooker "pepper steak" roast

Ingredients

3 cups of beef broth

2 red of pepper

4 small red onions

2 garlic clove

2 sirloin tip roast

½ cup of organic tamari sauce

2 green pepper

Fresh ground pepper

Directions:

1. First, you place the roast into the crock pot, grind pepper on top of roast as much or as little as you like.
2. After which you roughly chop up peppers and onions, place over top of the roast.
3. After that, you add broth and tamari sauce and clove of garlic.
4. Then you cover and cook in the crock pot on high for 4 hours.
5. Finally, you serve with your favorite garden veggies and voila!!

Slow Cooker Pot Roast with Shallots and Baby Carrots
Ingredients

28 baby carrots, peeled (or better still 10 large carrots cut into thirds)

Sea salt

Herbs de Provence

1 cup of beef broth

Butter, ghee (or better still coconut oil)

2- 6 lb. of Chuck Roast

16 shallots (peeled)

Freshly ground pepper (I prefer a battery operated grinder so I have one hand free to handle the roast)

Garlic powder

½ cup of red wine (it is optional-but gives a richer flavor)

Directions:

1. First, you generously season roast with sea salt, pepper, garlic powder and herbs de Provence.
2. After which you heat a cast iron pan on med/high heat.
3. Then when the pan is hot adding enough butter, ghee or coconut oil to lightly coat the bottom on the pan.
4. After that, you place roast in pan and brown the first side, turn over and brown the second side (usually about 4-5 minutes a side) then place meat in slow cooker, add broth and wine.
5. Then you add shallots and carrots to crock pot, sprinkle with sea salt, freshly ground pepper and herbs de Provence.
6. Finally, you place lid on crock pot and cook either 4 hours on high or 8 hours on low.
7. After that, you carve beef against the grain and serve.

Micronutrient Diet Recipes

Slow Cooker Roast, Potatoes, and Carrots

Tips:

This is a classic one dish roast dinner simplified by the slow cooker.

Ingredients

4-5 red potatoes (scrubbed and quartered)

3-4 carrots (peeled and chopped into 2 inch pieces)

2 teaspoons of sea salt

1-1/2 teaspoon of oregano

½ cup of beef stock (or better still water)

Salt and pepper (to taste)

1 4-5 lb of beef roast (remember any kind will work although I prefer chuck)

1 onion (skin removed and quartered)

2 cloves garlic (crushed or minced)

½ teaspoon of pepper

½ teaspoon of thyme

2 tablespoons of butter

2 tablespoons of flour, gluten free flour, non-GMO cornstarch or better still arrowroot powder

Directions:

1. First, you place roast in crockpot.
2. After which you sprinkle 1 teaspoon of salt over one side of the roast.
3. After that, you flip it over and sprinkle the other side of the roast with the remaining 1 teaspoon of salt.

4. At this point, you add garlic, oregano, and thyme evenly over the meat.
5. Then you tuck the onion quarters, carrots and potatoes around the roast.
6. Furthermore, you add ½ cup beef stock/water and turn on low for about 8 hours or high for 5 hours.
7. Then after time has elapsed, you remove roast, potatoes and carrots from crockpot and place on a platter to cool.

If you want to make a gravy

1. First strain your liquid still in the crockpot with a fine mesh strainer.
2. After which you set strained liquid aside.
3. After that, you melt 2 tablespoons of butter in a small saucepan over medium heat.
4. Then you add 2 tablespoons of flour of choice and whisk to create a roux.
5. At this point, you cook for about 1-2 minutes. (Please See Note below for gluten free version)
6. This is when you add reserved strained liquid to roux, whisking to prevent lumps.
7. In addition, you simmer until thickened.
8. After which you taste test and adjust seasonings if needed.
9. Finally, you slice your roast and serve with hot gravy and vegetables on the side.

Note:

1. For gluten free gravy, I suggest you add strained gravy to a small saucepan.
2. After which you heat until beginning to bubble.
3. After that, you make a slurry with cornstarch or arrowroot powder and a small amount of water.
4. Then you pour into hot liquid and whisk until thickened.

5. Finally, you season with salt and pepper.
6. Remember that arrowroot does best when added right at the end (It can lose thickening power the longer it cooks).

Slow cooker Crabapple & Pepper Jelly

Ingredients

2 small jalapeno pepper (preferably, chopped and seeded)

3 cups of vinegar

4 tablespoons of maple syrup

4 regular green peppers (preferably, chopped and seeded)

4 cups of crabapples (make sure you cut in half and cored)

1 ½ cup of sugar

Directions:

1. First, you toss all the ingredients in a slow cooker.
2. After which you cook on high for 3-4 hours, then let simmer on low for another hour.
3. After that, you place mixture in food processor or blender.
4. Then you place mixture (while it is still hot) in a sterilized jar and place in fridge or if you'd like to freeze it remember not to fill all the way to the top.
5. Remember, if you'd like you can process jar in hot water for an additional 5 minutes.
6. Enjoy!

Strawberry Lavender Chia Jam (Pectin & Sugar Free)

Ingredients:

4 tablespoons of Culinary Lavender (wrap in cheesecloth)

1 Tablespoon of Sweet Leaf Stevia Extract

3 quarts Strawberries (I prefer fresh picked, I am sure you could sub with frozen)

½ Lemon (should be squeezed over strawberries in layers, adds acidity and helps retain color)

2 Tablespoons of Chia seeds

Directions:

1. First, you hull 3 qts strawberries and put in crockpot on low.
2. After which you drizzle each layer with lemon juice as you fill up the Crockpot.
3. After that, you fill cheesecloth square with 4 Tablespoons of culinary lavender, tie together and place in crockpot with berries.
4. Then you let cook for about 90 min. then you pour contents into blender (remove lavender pouch) and give a quick whirl.
5. Remember, if you do not have a blender, I suggest you chop berries before putting in CP and then use a potato masher to blend berries.
6. At this point, you place berries and lavender back in CP, add 2 Tablespoons of Chia seeds.
7. This is when you leave the cover askew to allow some liquid evaporation and cook another hour.
8. Furthermore, you turn off heat, add stevia, remove lavender pouch and pack into sterile jars.
9. Then from here you can use a hot water bath to seal jars or you can pop them in the freezer, either way, you will be happy to have it on hand.

15 DELECTABLE MICRONUTRIENT VEGAN RECIPES

Scrambled Eggs with Avocado, Onion and Cheddar

INGREDIENTS:

1 firm-ripe California avocado

1 1/3 cups of grated extra-sharp Cheddar (about 4 ounces)

2 small onion

8 large eggs

4 teaspoons of unsalted butter

Chopped fresh cilantro sprigs for garnish

Directions:

1. First, you chop onion, halve, pit, and peel avocado and cut into 1/4-inch pieces.
2. After which you whisk together eggs and Cheddar in a bowl.
3. After that, you season with salt and pepper.
4. At this point, you heat butter in a nonstick skillet over moderately high heat until foam subsides and sauté onion, stirring, about 2 minutes until just beginning to soften.
5. Then you add egg mixture and cook, stirring constantly, for about 1 minute until eggs are just set.
6. Furthermore, you remove skillet from heat and stir in avocado.
7. Finally, you serve eggs garnished with cilantro.

Edamame Salad with Avocado and Radishes

Ingredients

2 cloves of garlic (minced)

4 teaspoons of honey (**NOTE**: if you do not eat honey, I suggest you substitute with cane sugar or agave)

4 tablespoons of lightly toasted sesame seeds

Juice of 2 lime

1 cup of sliced green onion

2 ripe Hass avocado (cubed)

2 (16-ounce) bag frozen shelled edamame (thawed)

2 teaspoons of grated fresh ginger

½ cup of rice wine vinegar

6 tablespoons of extra virgin olive oil

Pinch of salt and freshly ground black pepper

6 tablespoons of chopped fresh parsley

10 to 16 small radishes (sliced)

Directions

1. First, you bring about 8 cups of water to boil, in a medium saucepan then add the edamame.
2. After which, you boil only for a couple of minutes — you want them cooked through but still firm.
3. After that, you drain the edamame and allow to cool to room temperature.
4. At this point, you whisk together the rice wine vinegar, ginger, oil, garlic, lime, honey, and salt and pepper in a small bowl (for me I prefer using an immersion blender to get the dressing

completely emulsified, but a fork or whisk and a strong arm will accomplish the same thing).
5. This is when you set your dressing aside.
6. Furthermore, you add the cooled edamame, parsley, avocado, green onion, radishes, and a sprinkling of sesame seeds.
7. After which you stir them gently together until combined.
8. Then you add the dressing a few large spoonful's at a time, tossing slightly between spoonful's, until you have the desired amount for your salad.
9. Finally, you serve and enjoy!

Avocado and Chickpea Salad Sandwiches

Yields: 8-12 sandwiches, depending on how big you make them

Ingredients

2 large ripe avocado

4 tablespoons of chopped green onion

Salt and pepper (to taste)

Fresh spinach leaves or preferably other sandwich toppings: lettuce, sprouts, tomato slices, etc.

2 (15-ounce) can chickpeas

½ cup of fresh cilantro (chopped)

Juice from 2 limes

Bread of your choice

Directions

1. First, you rinse and drain the chickpeas.
2. After which you add them to a large bowl.
3. After that you pit the avocado and using your knife, score the flesh to make cubes.
4. Then you scoop the cubes out of the skin with a spoon.
5. Furthermore, you use a sturdy fork or a potato masher, smash the chickpeas and avocado together.
6. At this point, you add cilantro, green onion, and lime juice to the mash and stir to thoroughly combine.
7. This is when you season with salt and pepper, to taste.

8. Spread the mixture on bread and top with your favorite sandwich toppings, to make it fun.
9. In addition, you can build a traditional sandwich with tomato, lettuce, cucumber and other goodies in the middle, or better still you can make them open-face with toppings like thinly sliced tomatoes, sprouts, jalapeños, lime zest, a slice of hard-boiled egg, or anything else you can think of.
10. Enjoy

Vegan Twist on the Classic Tuna Sandwich

Ingredients

6 tablespoons of Ann's Brussels Sprouts Relish

4 stalks celery (chopped)

2 cups of cashew cream

6 cups of water

2 (8-ounce) can garbanzo beans

½ cup of minced red onion

4 teaspoons of ground mustard seed

2 (8 ounces) of raw unsalted cashews

Directions

1. First, you drain and wash garbanzo beans and let them dry.
2. After which, you mash the beans with a fork.
3. After that, you chop the celery stalks.
4. If you want to make the cashew cream, I suggest you soak cashews in 6 cups of water.
5. At this point, you drain and reserve water.
6. Then you puree cashews adding about ½ cup of reserved water to create desired consistency.
7. This is when you mix in cashew cream, celery, mustard, onion and relish.
8. Finally, you garnish with sprouts, lettuce, tomatoes and radishes!

Mango Avocado Salad

Ingredients

4 avocados (cubed)

¼ cup of Cilantro Lime Dressing

4 mangos (cubed)

½ cup of red cabbage (chopped)

Directions:

1. The first thing you do is to cube your mangos.
2. After which you basically do the same thing to the avocado.
3. However, to consider with the avocados for this recipe: you want them to be just ripe. If they are overly ripe, they will get all mushy when you are tossing the salad.
4. At this point, you add the 4 mangos cubed, 4 avocados cubed, ½ cup chopped red cabbage and half of the dressing.
5. After that, you toss it lightly, adding more dressing if desired.
6. Enjoy!

Micronutrient Diet Recipes

Avocado and Cucumber Salad with Cilantro-Ginger Dressing

Ingredients

½ cup of cilantro leaves (chopped)

12 cloves garlic (crushed)

4 large cucumbers (chopped in 1/2-inch cubes)

8 celery stalks (thinly sliced on a diagonal)

4 avocados (halved, pitted and sliced)

2 medium tomato, sliced (it is optional)

2 bunch cilantro (leaves left on sprigs)

½ cup of ginger (peeled and chopped)

2 tablespoons of extra-virgin olive oil

2 teaspoons of fine sea salt

4 tablespoons of freshly squeezed lime juice

½ cup of fresh basil leaves (sliced)

Directions

1. First, you combine cilantro sprigs, ginger, olive oil and garlic in a bowl.
2. After which you muddle together until everything is well mashed.
3. After that, you add cucumbers and 2 teaspoons of salt.
4. This is when you stir to mix, cover the bowl and set it aside, stirring occasionally, for about 35 minutes.
5. At this point, you uncover the bowl and discard the cilantro sprigs.
6. Then you mix in celery and lime juice.
7. Furthermore, you season with more salt, if desired.

Micronutrient Diet Recipes

8. If you want to serve, I suggest you divide the avocado and optional tomato slices on the plates.
9. After that, you spoon the cucumber salad over the slices.
10. Finally, you garnish with the chopped cilantro and basil.
11. Then you serve and enjoy!

Tuscan White Bean Soup
Ingredients

2 small yellow onions (finely chopped)

8 garlic cloves (minced)

2 teaspoons of dried thyme

2 teaspoons of dried ground sage

4 tomatoes (seeded and chopped)

2 can cannellini beans (drained and rinsed)

2 pinches of salt and pepper, to taste

4 tablespoons of extra virgin olive oil

4 stalks celery stalk (diced)

4 teaspoons of dried oregano

2 teaspoons of dried basil

4 carrots (diced)

10 cups of vegetable stock

2 tablespoons of finely chopped sage (for garnish)

Directions

1. First, you heat the olive oil in a large pot over medium-high heat.
2. After which you add the onion, celery, and garlic.
3. After that, you cook these for about 3 minutes or until the onions turn translucent.
4. Then you add the basil, sage, oregano, thyme, carrots and tomatoes and stir to combine.

Micronutrient Diet Recipes

5. At this point, you cook for about 5 minutes, stirring occasionally.
6. Furthermore, you add the vegetable stock and cannellini beans, and bring the soup to a simmer.
7. After which you simmer for about 10 minutes, stirring occasionally.
8. This is when you place ½ of the soup in a blender and blend until creamy.
9. Then you return it to the pot and stir well to incorporate it.
10. In addition, you taste, and add salt and pepper as necessary.
11. Finally, you ladle the soup into bowls and garnish with a few leaves of fresh sage or basil.
12. Enjoy!

Mushroom soup with White Beans

Ingredients:
2 tablespoons of olive oil

2 small onion (finely chopped)

2 tablespoons of flour

2 cups of white beans

Salt and Pepper to taste

1 ¼ lb. of mushrooms (about 8 cups)

2 tablespoons of butter

2 - 4 cloves garlic (minced)

8 cups of vegetable stock

1 cup of half and half (or preferably whipping cream)

Directions:
1. First, you clean the mushrooms and slice half of them.
2. After which you finely chop the other half.
3. After that, heat the olive oil in a large saucepan set over medium-high heat and add the butter.
4. Then when the foam subsides, you add the onion, garlic, and both sliced and chopped mushrooms.
5. Furthermore, you reduce the heat slightly and sauté until the moisture evaporates and the mushrooms begin to turn golden.
6. Then you add the flour and cook, stirring to coat the mushrooms, for another minute.

Micronutrient Diet Recipes

7. In addition, you add the stock and beans and bring to a simmer.
8. At this point, you reduce the heat to low and cook for about 15 minutes.
9. Finally, you turn off the heat and stir in the cream.
10. After which you season with salt and pepper and serve immediately.
11. Enjoy!

Micronutrient Diet Recipes

Chickpeas Simmered in Masala Sauce

Ingredients

1 ¼ teaspoons of whole cumin seeds

2 teaspoons of finely grated fresh ginger

2/3 teaspoon of cayenne pepper

2 cups of finely chopped tomatoes

2 teaspoons of fine sea salt

2 teaspoons of lemon juice

6 tablespoons of extra virgin olive oil

2 cups of finely chopped onions

1 ¼ teaspoons of ground coriander

½ teaspoons of ground turmeric

2 cups of water

5 cups of cooked, drained chickpeas

1 teaspoon of garam masala

Directions

1. First, you heat the olive oil, in a frying pan over medium heat then add in the cumin seeds.
2. After which you give them a stir and let them toast for about 10 seconds.
3. After that, you add in the onions, stir them and fry until they begin to turn brown at the edges.
4. This is when you add the ginger, cayenne, coriander, and turmeric and give the spices a quick stir to combine them all with the onion.

Micronutrient Diet Recipes

5. At this point, you add in the tomatoes, water and salt.
6. Then you stir to combine everything and bring the mixture to a boil.
7. Furthermore, you cover the pan, turn the heat to low, and let the mixture simmer for about 10 minutes.
8. After that, you add in the chickpeas and bring the mixture back up to a boil.
9. Then you turn the heat back down to low, cover and let simmer for about 15 minutes.
10. Finally, you add the garam masala and lemon juice, stir it in, and let it all cook uncovered for another 5 minutes or so.

NOTE: You can enjoy this dish on its own or better still you can serve it over a bed of steamed rice.

Fingerling Potato Salad with Green Chili-Cilantro Salsa

Ingredients:
8 tablespoons of cider vinegar
4 cups of fresh cilantro sprigs (coarsely chopped)
½ cup of extra-virgin olive oil

8 lb. of fingerling potatoes (or preferably other small boiling potatoes)

6 fresh jalapeño chills (with seeds and ribs removed from 4 of them)

3 shallots (coarsely chopped)

2 garlic clove (coarsely chopped)

Directions:

1. First, you cover potatoes with salted cold water by 1 inch, then simmer for about 10 to 15 minutes until just tender,
2. After which you drain potatoes and rinse under cold water until slightly cooled.
3. After that, you halve lengthwise and while still warm gently toss with 2 tablespoons of vinegar.
4. At this point, your cool potatoes to room temperature, then season with salt and pepper.
5. Then while potatoes cook, you coarsely chop jalapeños and pulse in a food processor with cilantro, shallots, garlic, oil, and remaining 6 tablespoons vinegar until finely chopped.
6. Finally, you toss potatoes with salsa and enjoy!

Five-minute vegan pancake

Ingredients

1 cups of sugar

1 teaspoon of baking soda

6 tablespoons of vegetable oil

1 cups of water

1 ½ cups of flour

3 tablespoons of cocoa

½ teaspoon of salt

1 teaspoons of vanilla

1 tablespoons of vinegar

Directions

1. First, you sift dry ingredients into an ungreased (8x8) pan.
2. After which you make 3 holes in dry ingredients.
3. In the first hole, you put 6 teaspoons of oil.
4. In the second hole, you put 1 teaspoon of vanilla.
5. In the third hole, you put 1 Tablespoon of vinegar.
6. After that, you pour 1 cup of water over all and stir until smooth.
7. Then you bake at a temperature of 350 degrees for 35 minutes.
8. Finally, you frost or sprinkle with confectioner's sugar.
9. Can double recipe if you wish.

Roasted Cauliflower & 16 Roasted Cloves of Garlic

Ingredients

16 garlic cloves (peeled and lightly crushed)

1 teaspoon of salt

More olive oil, to drizzle if you wish

1 large cauliflower (it should be trimmed and cut into bite size pieces, washed with water still on)

1-2 teaspoons of minced fresh rosemary

¼-½ teaspoon of black pepper

¼ cup olive oil, (adding more to taste)

Directions

1. First, you mix oil, rosemary, salt, pepper and garlic together.
2. After which you toss in cauliflower and place in a large casserole dish in one layer.
3. After that, you roast in a preheated oven at a temperature of 450 degrees for 20 minutes.
4. Then you give a toss and bake for about 10 more minutes.

Roasted Green Beans
Ingredients

1 -2 tablespoons of olive oil (or preferably just enough to lightly coat beans)

½ teaspoon of fresh ground pepper (or preferably to taste, omit if using Mrs. Dash)

2 lbs. of green beans

1 teaspoon of kosher salt (or preferably to taste, may substitute with Mrs. Dash if desired)

Directions

1. Meanwhile, you heat oven to a temperature of 400°F.
2. After which you wash, dry well, and trim green beans.
3. After that, you put green beans on a jelly roll pan.
4. Then you drizzle with olive oil and sprinkle with salt and pepper to taste (I prefer them salty so I use about 1 1/2 teaspoons of salt and about 8-10 grinds of the pepper mill).

Note: Mrs. Dash may be a good substituted for salt and pepper as desired.

5. At this point, you use your hands to be sure all the beans are evenly coated and spread them out into 1 layer.
6. Furthermore, you roast for about 20-25 minutes, turning after 15 minutes, until beans are fairly brown in spots and somewhat shriveled.
7. Finally, you serve hot or at room temperature.

Vegetarian Lasagna
Ingredients

½ cup of grated carrot

6 cooked lasagna noodles

1 (16 ounce) package frozen chopped spinach (thawed and well drained)

1 ½ cups of thinly sliced zucchini

½ cup of grated parmesan cheese

1 ½ quarts spaghetti sauce (or better still your favorite homemade or jar spaghetti sauce)

½ teaspoon of oregano

1 (16 ounce) container ricotta cheese

2 eggs

1 cups of sliced fresh mushrooms

3 cups of shredded part-skim mozzarella cheese

Directions

1. First, you mix carrots, oregano, and spaghetti sauce together.
2. After that, you mix Ricotta, spinach, and eggs together in separate bowl.
3. Then you spread ½ cup spaghetti sauce in bottom of 9 x 13-inch baking dish.
4. After which you layer 3 lasagna noodles, ½ remaining sauce, ½ sliced zucchini, ½ Ricotta mixture, ½ Mozzarella, ½ sliced mushrooms, and ½ Parmesan.
5. At this point, you repeat layers with remaining ingredients.
6. Bake in a temperature of 350 degrees' oven for about 45 minutes.

Vegetarian Split Pea Soup

Ingredients

14 cups of water (or 14 cups vegetable stock)

4 teaspoons of salt

4 cups of onions (minced)

6 stalks celery (minced)

2 potatoes (diced)

2-8 tablespoons of balsamic vinegar, to taste (or preferably red wine vinegar)

6 cups of dried split peas

2 bay leaf

2 teaspoons of dry mustard

8 medium garlic cloves (minced)

4 medium carrots (sliced)

Fresh ground black pepper

Optional toppings

Fresh ripe tomatoes, diced (it is optional)

Fresh parsley, minced (it is optional)

Sesame oil (it is optional)

Directions

1. First, you place the dried split peas, water or vegetable stock, bay leaf, salt and mustard in a large pot.

2. After which you bring to a boil, reduce heat to low, and simmer, partially covered for about 20 minutes, stirring occasionally to prevent split peas from sticking to bottom of pot.
3. After that, you add onions, carrots, garlic, celery, and potato. (NOTE: You can sauté these first or better still add them in directly if you want a fat free soup).
4. At this point, you partially cover and allow to simmer for about 40 minutes, stirring occasionally (NOTE: You may need to add extra water).
5. Then you season to taste with pepper and vinegar.
6. Finally, you serve with a drizzle of sesame oil, diced tomato and minced parsley.

CONCLUSION

These Micronutrient Miracle Diet program would help you lose weight and prevent and reverse common disorders, including obesity, heart disease, and diabetes. Get in shape and live a healthier lifestyle this Season taking this Micronutrient recipe.

If you follow religiously to the "MICRONUTRIENT MIRACLE" By Jayson B. Calton Ph.D. and Mira Calton CN and some of the recipes outlined in this book. You are going to be seeing results in 22 days, because it is proven to work.

Thanks

However, if you enjoyed the recipes in this book, please take the time to share your thoughts and post a positive review with 5-star rating on Amazon, it would make me serve you better. It'd be greatly appreciated!

Thank you and good luck!

www.ingramcontent.com/pod-product-compliance
Lightning Source LLC
Chambersburg PA
CBHW081726100526
44591CB00016B/2519